THE FUNNIEST FOOTBALL CHANTS... EVER!

Also available

The Funniest England Quotes... Ever!

The Funniest Liverpool Quotes... Ever!

The Funniest Chelsea Quotes... Ever!

The Funniest West Ham Quotes... Ever!

The Funniest Spurs Quotes... Ever!

The Funniest Arsenal Quotes... Ever!

The Funniest Man City Quotes... Ever!

The Funniest Newcastle Quotes... Ever!

The Funniest United Quotes... Ever!

The Funniest Leeds Quotes... Ever!

The Funniest Boro Quotes... Ever!

The Funniest Forest Quotes... Ever!

The Funniest Sunderland Quotes... Ever!

The Funniest Leicester Quotes... Ever!

The Funniest Saints Quotes... Ever!

The Funniest Everton Quotes... Ever!

The Funniest Villa Quotes... Ever!

The Funniest QPR Quotes... Ever!

The Funniest Celtic Quotes... Ever!

The Funniest Rangers Quotes... Ever!

"If they made a film of my life, I think they should get George Clooney to play me."

THE FUNNIEST FOOTBALL QUOTES... EVER!

"Mario woke up this morning with a hardening – in his thigh!"

by Gordon Law

Copyright © 2023 by Eagle Books.

No part of this publication may be reproduced, stored in a retrieval system or transmitted in any form by any means, electronic, mechanical, photocopying, or otherwise, without prior written permission of the publisher Eagle Books.

contact@gmediagroup.co.uk

ISBN: 978-1-917744-18-8
Imprint: Eagle Books

Photo courtesy of: Shutterstock.com/Maxisport

Contents

Arsenal..................6	Newcastle..............52
Aston Villa................9	Forest....................56
Bournemouth..........13	Southampton..........58
Brentford................15	Tottenham..............61
Brighton..................18	West Ham..............64
Chelsea..................21	Wolves...................67
Crystal Palace........25	Celtic.....................69
Everton...................28	Rangers.................72
Fulham...................31	More clubs.............75
Leeds.....................35	England.................85
Leicester................39	N. Ireland..............88
Liverpool................41	Rep. Ireland...........91
Man City................45	Scotland................94
Man Utd.................49	Wales....................97

THE FUNNIEST FOOTBALL CHANTS... EVER!

ARSENAL

"He's tall, he's quick, his name's a porno flick. Emmanuel, Emmanuel."

A ditty for Emmanuel Petit

"You're not fit to referee!"

Chant for ref Mark Clattenburg who was being treated for an injury

"Let's talk about Cesc baby. Let's talk about Flamini. Let's talk about Theo Walcott, Freddie Ljungberg and Henry. Let's talk about Cesc!"

A catchy song to the tune of 'Let's Talk About Sex'

THE FUNNIEST FOOTBALL CHANTS... EVER!

"Di-mi-tar, Di-mi-tar. His mum washes cars. On the North Cir-cu-lar."

To Spurs' Bulgarian star Dimitar Berbatov

"Osama, woooah. Osama, woooah. He follows Arsenal. He's hiding in Kabul."

Chant for Osama bin Laden, a reported Gunners fan

"Lasagne, woooah. Lasagne, woooah. We laughed ourselves to bits. When Tottenham got the sh*ts!"

After Spurs missed out on the top four when six players had food poisoning

THE FUNNIEST FOOTBALL CHANTS... EVER!

"One Song. We've only got one Song!"

Hailing midfielder Alex Song

"You're just a fat Eddie Murphy!"

Gunners fans to Jimmy Floyd Hasselbaink

"He's bald. He's sh*t. He plays when no-one's fit. Pascal Cygan, Pascal Cygan!"

The fans love him really

"Green in a minute. He's going green in a minute"

At Highbury after FC Porto brought on a substitute called... Hulk

THE FUNNIEST FOOTBALL CHANTS... EVER!

"One Lily Savage, there's only one Lily Savage."

Directed at Blackburn's Robbie Savage

"You'd better watch out, you'd better not cry. You'd better be good I'm telling you why. Cos Santi C is coming to town."

A festive chant for midfielder Santi Cazorla

ASTON VILLA

"Juan Pablo Angel. There's only Juan Pablo Angel."

Chant with a clever play on words

THE FUNNIEST FOOTBALL CHANTS... EVER!

"You put your right glove on, your left glove on. You play for Aston Villa and you're number one. You do the Aussie Bozzie and you turn around. That's what it's all about."

Mark Bosnich gets his 'Hokey Cokey' song

"He's fat, he's round, he's never spent a pound. Doug Ellis, Doug Ellis."

Aimed at the frugal chairman

"Time for a sandwich, it must be time for a sandwich."

The away faithful spotting Man United fans leaving their seats early for refreshment

THE FUNNIEST FOOTBALL CHANTS... EVER!

"Start spreading the news, he's playing today. I want to see him score again – Dwight Yorke, Dwight Yorke. If he can score from there, he'll score from anywhere. It's up to you, Dwight Yorke, Dwight Yorke."

Saluting Dwight Yorke to the tune of 'New York, New York'

"Feed the Hare and he will score!"

Aston Villa fans to Marlon Harewood

"Randy, Randy, buy 'em a roof."

To chairman Randy Lerner on the roofless terrace at Gillingham

THE FUNNIEST FOOTBALL CHANTS... EVER!

"Oh Carlos Cuellar, you are the love of my life. Oh Carlos Cuellar, I'd let you sh*g my wife. Oh Carlos Cuellar, I want curly hair too!"

A tribute to Carlos Cuellar to the tune of 'I Love You Baby'

"John Carew, Carew. He likes a lap-dance or two. He might even pay for you. John Carew, Carew."

After Carew had visited a gentlemen's club

"Forest Gump is a Villa Fan! Forest Gump is a Villa Fan!"

On reports that Hollywood actor Tom Hanks was a supporter

THE FUNNIEST FOOTBALL CHANTS... EVER!

BOURNEMOUTH

"He's big. He's quick. He's got a 12-inch dick. Super Fletch. Super Fletch."
On club legend Steve Fletcher

"Your sister is your mother. Your father is your brother. You all sh*g one another. The Blackburn family."
To the tune of the Addams Family song

"You're not famous. You're not famous. You're not famous anymore. You're not famous anymore..."
Chanting at Leeds United

"What a waste of petrol! What a waste of petrol!"

To visiting teams who made the long trek to the south coast

"Dom Solanke. He used to be Scouse. Now he's got a seaside house. 20 million down the drain. Dom Solanke scores again."

A ditty for striker Dominic Solanke

"Oh when the Saints go Johnstone's Paints. Oh when the Saints go Johnstone's Paints…"

Mocking Southampton's relegation to the third tier

THE FUNNIEST FOOTBALL CHANTS... EVER!

"Does the social know you're here?"

When visiting northern England teams

"If you can't talk proper, shut your mouth!"

To Leeds fans, without any irony

BRENTFORD

"Vauxhall, Vauxhall Motors. They're the greatest team in history. From some plant in Ellesmere. They knocked Rangers out on penalties!"

Having a swipe at QPR, to the Flintstones theme

THE FUNNIEST FOOTBALL CHANTS... EVER!

"Premiership side you're having a laugh. All you've got is a Premiership bath. Premiership side, you're having a laugh. All you've got up front, is a big giraffe."

Away at Southampton with a dig at striker Peter Crouch

"We're just a bus stop in Hounslow!"

Flipping a chant from rival fans on its head

"Bees up, Luton down."

Sang after winning promotion and Luton were relegated, to the tune of 'Knees Up Mother Brown'

THE FUNNIEST FOOTBALL CHANTS... EVER!

"Put him down, put him down, put him down!"

Aimed at an injured Kurt Zouma who admitted to kicking his cat

"Ronny Noades, Ronny Noades, Ronny Ronny Noades. He's got white hair, he's a millionaire. Ronny Ronny Noades."

A chant for chairman Ron Noades to the Boney M tune

"Diego woooah! Diego woooah! He came from Uruguay. He made the Fulham cry."

After Diego Forlan's goal for Atletico Madrid ended Fulham's Euro adventure

THE FUNNIEST FOOTBALL CHANTS... EVER!

"1-0 to the taxi boys. 1-0 to the taxi boys..."

Response to opposition fans' chant of "come in a taxi" after Bees scored

"We pay your benefits. We pay your benefits..."

A chant for every northern club

BRIGHTON

"Cody Gakpo, he's one of our own."

After Chelsea's scoreboard identified Liverpool's Cody Gakpo as one of the Brighton players

THE FUNNIEST FOOTBALL CHANTS... EVER!

"We've got tiny Cox. Say, we've got tiny Cox."

Chanted after 5ft 3in midfielder Dean Cox scored

"When the ball hits the goal. It's not Shearer or Cole. That's Zamora!"

A tribute to Bobby Zamora to the tune of 'Amore'

"He's fat, he's round. He's given us a ground. John Prescott, John Prescott."

After the deputy prime minister approved the new Amex stadium

THE FUNNIEST FOOTBALL CHANTS... EVER!

"Tw*t in a bear suit. You're just a tw*t in a bear suit!"

Sung at Blackpool mascot Bloomfield Bear after he removed his head

"Tony Bloom, went to Europe in a brand new Skoda. Brought us back a magic man. Jakub, Jakub Moder."

An ode to the Polish midfielder

"Michel Kuipers, he's a former Dutch marine. A former Dutch marine. A former Dutch marine."

The keeper gets the 'Yellow Submarine' treatment

THE FUNNIEST FOOTBALL CHANTS... EVER!

"We're supposed to be at home!"

Seagulls fans on being forced to play home games at Priestfield Stadium

"Bexhill, it's just like watching Bexhill."

During a loss at Southend

CHELSEA

"Oh the weather outside is frightful, but the goals are so delightful. Stamford Bridge is the place to go. Mourinho, Mourinho, Mourinho."

Chelsea fans' festive chant about their manager

THE FUNNIEST FOOTBALL CHANTS... EVER!

"He's now a Blue, he was a Red, Torres Torres. He left the Kop to join the Shed, Torres Torres. He used to go out on the rob. But now he's got a proper job. Fernando Torres, Chelsea's number nine!"

The fans are thrilled with their new striker

"Cech has got his hat on. Hip hip hip hooray. Cech has got his hat on. You're not gonna score today."

Chelsea supporters love a nursery rhyme

"You're shish, and you know you are."

Turkish side Galatasaray are welcomed to Stamford Bridge

THE FUNNIEST FOOTBALL CHANTS... EVER!

"The sh*t from Spurs, they booked his flight. But Willian, he saw the light. He got a call from Abramovich, and off he went to Stamford Bridge. He hates Tottenham, he hates Tottenham. He hates Tottenham and he hates Tottenham!"

Willian chose to sign for Chelsea over Spurs despite completing a medical there

"He's got bird sh*t on his head! He's got bird sh*t on his head!"

Laughing at Djibril Cisse's haircut

"We were here when you were good."

Chelsea fans at Old Trafford

THE FUNNIEST FOOTBALL CHANTS... EVER!

"Chelsea wherever you may be, keep your wife from John Terry."

After the defender's alleged affair with Wayne Bridge's ex-girlfriend

"We'll just call you Dave. We'll just call you Dave. Azpilicueta. We'll just call you Dave."

The fans struggle with the Spaniard's name

"He's here, he's there, we're not allowed to swear. Frank Leboeuf, Frank Leboeuf."

The defender had asked the fans not to curse when singing his name

CRYSTAL PALACE

"Oh Moses, woooah! Oh Moses, woooah! He comes from Norbury, he parted the Red Sea!"

Fans salute winger Victor Moses

"Brucie the Elephant packed his cash, and said goodbye to the Palace. Off he went like a greedy fat lump. C*nt, c*nt, c*nt!"

After the manager walked out on the club, to the tune of 'Nellie the Elephant'

"Patrick Vieira, he's won more than you."

Palace fans take aim at their Tottenham counterparts

THE FUNNIEST FOOTBALL CHANTS... EVER!

"N'Diaye-e-i will always love you-oo-oo-oo-ou!"

Alassane N'Diaye gets a love song

"Oh Luka, woooah! Oh Luka, woooah! He comes from Serbia. He'll f*cking murder ya!"

A chant for Eagles midfield hard man Luka Milivojevic

"Terry Venables walks on water. Everybody knows that dog sh*t floats!"

The former manager is not much-loved

"Mason Greenwood, he's one of your own!"

Palace fans taunt the Man United faithful

THE FUNNIEST FOOTBALL CHANTS... EVER!

"Your dad's a cucumber!... You should've stayed in a burger!"

Directed at Colchester keeper Dean Gerken

"Just one Lombardo, give him to me. He's from Juventus, in Italy. He's got no hair, but we don't care. We've got Lombardo. From Italy! Lombardo! Lombardo! Lombardo!"

To the tune of 'Just one Cornetto'

"We've got that Terry Phelan. We've got that Terry Phelan. We've got that Terry Phelan. On loan, loan, loan. Woooah!"

A song about the defender, to the tune of 'You've Lost That Lovin' Feeling'

EVERTON

"He's Brazilian. He only cost £50 million. And we think he's f*cking brilliant. Richarlison."
A song for Richarlison to the theme of 'She's Electric' by Oasis

"Tim Timminy, Tim Timminy, Tim Tim Teroo. We've got Tim Howard and he says f*ck you!"
Fans celebrate their Tourettes-suffering keeper in the tune of 'Chim Chiminey'

"He's big, he's tall, he's clumsy on the ball. Peter Crouch."
A chant for the lanky striker

THE FUNNIEST FOOTBALL CHANTS... EVER!

"Get that kid on from Barcelona. He must be better than that lad Kone. Gerard De-something from Barcelona. I can't pronounce it, what's his name?"

Gerard Deulofeu's song to the theme of 'Amarillo'

"World Cup – and you f*cked it up! World Cup..."

Aimed at referee Graham Poll after he gave three yellow cards at the 2006 Finals

"He's quick, he's game. We can't pronounce his name. Russian lad. Russian lad."

Diniyar Bilyaletdinov gets his own song

THE FUNNIEST FOOTBALL CHANTS... EVER!

"Martinez said he's not for sale and I am satisfied. Chelsea want those diamond rings that money just can't buy. I don't care too much for money, money can't buy you Stones. Can't buy me Stoooooones, money can't buy you Stones. Can't buy me Stoooooones, money can't buy you Stones."

A chant for John Stones who was attracting interest from Chelsea to the tune of 'Money Can't Buy Me Love'

"Leighton Baines, you probably think this song is about you!"

The defender's chant, to the tune of Carly Simon's 'You're So Vain'

THE FUNNIEST FOOTBALL CHANTS... EVER!

"He's six foot five and his name's Yerry Mina. His cock's like the hose on a vacuum cleaner. He goes on the lemo with David Ospina. Heyyy Yerry Mina."

A 'Macarena' tribute to the centre half

"The baby's not yours. The baby's not yours. Steven Gerrard. The baby's not yours."

The fans respond to newspaper speculation about the Reds midfielder

FULHAM

"Dicks out! Dicks out!"

A chant for manager Alan Dicks

THE FUNNIEST FOOTBALL CHANTS... EVER!

"We've got Seol! Seol! Always believe in your Seol. You've got the power to know. You're indestructible. Always believe it…"

A song for South Korean Seol Ki-Hyeon to the tune of 'Gold'

"You'll never shop at Harrods. You'll never shop at Harrods."

Fulham fans like to frequent the luxury store owned by their chairman Mohamed Al-Fayed

"Made of Lego, your ground is made of Lego."

Sang at Chester's Deva Stadium

THE FUNNIEST FOOTBALL CHANTS... EVER!

"We've won it one time. We've won it one time. The Intertoto. We've won it one time."

The fans have a laugh at themselves

"We're forever reaching finals, reaching finals in Hamburg. We'll be on the beer while they'll be stuck here. Watching EastEnders with their old dear. We'll be on the Reeperbahn, they'll still be in Dagenham. We're forever reaching finals, reaching finals in Hamburg!"

Responding to West Ham's 'Bubbles' chant

"You only live around the corner."

Aimed at Manchester United fans at Craven Cottage

THE FUNNIEST FOOTBALL CHANTS... EVER!

"One man couldn't carry. Carry! Couldn't carry Lampard. What? One man and his pick-up truck couldn't carry Lampard. Two men..."

Mocking Frank Lampard's weight

"Jimmy Bullard Bullard. He's better than Steve Gerrard. He's slimmer than Frank Lampard. Jimmy Bullard Bullard."

The Whites midfielder is lauded by the weight-conscious fans

"Al-Fayed – wooah. Al-Fayed – wooah. He wants to be a Brit and QPR are sh*t."

When owner Mohamed Al-Fayed had trouble applying for a passport

LEEDS

"He's here, he's there, he wears no underwear, Lee Bowyer, Lee Bowyer."

After the midfielder revealed he likes to go 'commando'

"Here for the shot-put, we're only here for the shot-put."

Leeds fans while losing 4-1 at Rotherham's Don Valley athletics stadium

"Face like a donkey, you've got a face like a donkey."

Aimed at United's Ruud van Nistelrooy

THE FUNNIEST FOOTBALL CHANTS... EVER!

"Wembley, Wembley. We're the famous Leeds United and we're off to win some paint!"

The supporters look on the bright side of relegation to League One and entry to the Johnstone's Paint Trophy

"We've got McAllister, you've got chlamydia."

Leeds fans at Peterborough where there were two mobile STI testing vans outside the ground

"Cellino... He comes from Italy – he don't pay VAT!"

An ode to the club's new owner, who failed to pay tax on an imported Range Rover

THE FUNNIEST FOOTBALL CHANTS... EVER!

"Town full of sea men, you're just a town full of sea men."

To Plymouth Argyle supporters

"Enoch has got a massive cock. Enoch, Enoch. Enoch has got a massive cock. Enoch, Enoch. He sh*gged a woman, now she's dead. He swings his cock around his head. Enoch Showunmi, United's 21."

An ode to the forward

"Ten men... We've only got 10 men..."

After a player from Leeds Ladies is subbed on in Lucas Radebe's testimonial

"You've lost Ndlovu and Whelan."

Taunting Coventry's fans to the tune of 'You've Lost That Loving Feeling'

"All of the spies. Were hidden away. Just try not to worry. You'll beat us some day. We beat you at home. We beat you away. Stop crying Frank Lampard..."

A 'Spygate' chant to the Oasis track 'Stop Crying Your Heart Out'

"You don't know what you're doing."

Leeds fans to a Derby supporter who proposed to his girlfriend during the game

THE FUNNIEST FOOTBALL CHANTS... EVER!

LEICESTER

"Do you work at B&Q? Do you work at B&Q?"

A DIY chant to the orange-clad fans of Blackpool

"Yuki, Yuki, Super Yuki Abe. He scores past the Forest, he scores past the Villa. He lives next door, to f*cking Godzilla. Yuki, Yuki Abe!"

Leicester fans' ode to Yuki Abe

"Who let the Frogs out? Who? Who? Who?"

Arsenal's team of Frenchmen are welcomed to the field

"I predict a Fryatt, I predict a Fryatt."

The fans give Matty Fryatt his Kaiser Chiefs inspired song

"Barry Hayles is bigger than this, he's got a door and a window. Barry Hayles is bigger than this."

Taunting Cardiff fans on their small Ninian Park ground

"Bus stop in Walsall. You're just a bus stop in Walsall. Bus stop in Walsall. You're just a bus stop in Walsall!"

Sung to the Wolves supporters

"I wanna go home, I wanna go home. Watford's a sh*thole. I wanna go home."

Foxes fans away at Vicarage Road

"Robin Hood, what a w*nker, what a w*nker!"

Mocking the Nottingham legend

"Does your missus know you're here?"

Blackburn love rat Garry Flitcroft gets stick

LIVERPOOL

"Who's the Scouser in the wig?"

Taunting Wayne Rooney's hair transplant

THE FUNNIEST FOOTBALL CHANTS... EVER!

"He's big, he's Red, his feet stick out the bed, Peter Crouch."

Paying tribute to lanky Reds forward

"Dirk Kuyt, as good as he may be. Hit every branch on the ugly tree. Like Fowler, Crouch and Craig Bellamy. Dirk Kuyt's boss, but he's f*cking ugly."

The attacker gets a unique song

"I'm your biggest fan, I'll follow you until you love me. Aqui, Aqui, Aquilani."

Alberto Aquilani gets praise from the fan base, to the tune of Lady Gaga's 'Paparazzi'

THE FUNNIEST FOOTBALL CHANTS... EVER!

"We thought his days were numbered. Now he plays here every week. We can't pronounce his surname, so we call him Nick the Greek."
An ode to Sotirios Kyrgiakos

"I've got the moves like Agger. I've got the moves like Agger. I've got the moves like Agger."
A ditty for Daniel Agger to the tune of 'Moves Like Jagger'

"Cilla wants her teeth back! Cilla wants her teeth back!"
To Barcelona's Ronaldinho, who probably wouldn't know who Cilla Black was

THE FUNNIEST FOOTBALL CHANTS... EVER!

"It's neat, it's weird. It's Rafa's goatee beard!"

The manager gets a facial hair song

"Oh well I wish I could watch Suarez every day. When the skills start flowing and he sticks a chance away. Oh I wish I could watch Suarez every day. Let the chants... Ring out... For Suarez."

Fans sing about their striker at Christmas, to the theme of 'I Wish It Could Be Christmas Everyday'

"Armani's number one!"

Reds fans after David James decided to go into modelling

THE FUNNIEST FOOTBALL CHANTS... EVER!

"Bjornebye in my gang, my gang, my gang. Bjornebye in my gang, oh yeah!"
A chant for the Norway defender (to the tune of 'I'm The Leader Of The Gang')

MAN CITY

"Sven, Sven, wherever you may be. You are the pride of Man City. You can sh*g my wife, on our settee... If we get to Wembley."
City fans give a nod to their 'lady's man' boss Sven-Goran Eriksson

"Next year, you'll be City fans."
Sang to fellow wealthy club Chelsea

"Singing Aye-Yi-Yippee Sun Jihai. Singing Aye-Yi-Yippee Sun Jihai. Singing Aye-Yi-Yippee, his dad owns a chippy. Aye-Yi-Yippee Sun Jihai."

Fans pay tribute to Chinese defender Sun Jihai... and his dad

"Niall Quinn's disco pants are the best, they go up from his a*se to his chest. They are better than Adam and the Ants. Niall Quinn's... disco pants."

Saluting the lanky forward

"Adebayor, Adebayor. He stamped on Van Persie. And slid on the floor."

He scored against his old team Arsenal

THE FUNNIEST FOOTBALL CHANTS... EVER!

"We used to have a song for you. Tevez, Tevez. But now you've gone from red to blue. Tevez, Tevez. We're sorry for the hurtful words. I bet you've sh*gged a load of birds. Carlos Tevez. City till he dies."

Fans conjure up new lyrics for the former Man United star

"And all the runs that Kinky makes are winding. And all the goals that City score are blinding. There are many times that we'd like to score again, but we don't know how. Cos maybe, you're gonna be the one that saves me. And after all, you're my Alan Ball."

The Oasis 'Wonderwall' tribute song

THE FUNNIEST FOOTBALL CHANTS... EVER!

"Don't sell Joe Hart, our super Joey Hart. I just don't think you'll understand. That if you sell Joe Hart, our super Joey Hart. You're gonna have a riot on your hands."

The supporters get behind their keeper

"Is this the Etihad?"

City fans poke fun at themselves with a Goodison Park chant

"Oh what a night! Watching City on a Wednesday night. You play Thursday 'cos you're f*cking sh*te! What a feeling, what a night!"

City fans remind United about their European success

MAN UNITED

"David James, superstar, drops more b*llocks than Grobbelaar."

Taunting the keeper during a 3-1 win at Liverpool

"You're not special anymore!"

To Jose Mourinho after United knocked Inter out of the Champions League

"This is how it feels to be City. This is how it feels to be small. This is how it feels when your team wins nothing at all."

Laughing at the then-struggling neighbours

"Park, Park, wherever you may be. You eat dogs in your home country. Could be worse, could be a Scouse. Eating rats in your council house."

United fans pay tribute to Ji-Sung Park

"Feed the Scousers. Let them know it's Christmas time!"

Having a laugh at Liverpool's expense

"His name is Rio and he dances on the grass. Don't take the ball from him, he'll kick your f*cking ass."

To the tune of Duran Duran's hit 'Rio'

THE FUNNIEST FOOTBALL CHANTS... EVER!

"Your teeth are offside, your teeth are offside. Luis Suarez, your teeth are offside."

Taking aim at the Liverpool forward

"You're Spurs, and you know you are!"

Sung by United fans to the Tottenham supporters

"We all agree, Jaap Stam is harder than Arnie!"

An amusing chant at Sturm Graz's Arnold Schwarzenegger Stadium in 2000

"You're just a town full of rugby."

The United away support at Hull City

THE FUNNIEST FOOTBALL CHANTS... EVER!

NEWCASTLE

"Liam O'Brien, Andy O'Brien. Any, any, any O'Brien. Who put the ball in the Mackems' net? O'Brien, O'Brien."

The goal scorers against Sunderland, to the tune of 'Any Old Iron'

"You stole my holiday!"

Sung at West Ham after their sponsors, travel firm XL, went bust

"You're not yodelling. You're not yodelling. You're not yodelling any more!"

Directed at FC Zurich fans in Switzerland

THE FUNNIEST FOOTBALL CHANTS... EVER!

"You put your left foot in. Your left foot out. In out, in out, you shake it all about. You do the Ameobi and you turn around. That's what it's all about. Woah! Shola Ameobi. Woah! Shola Ameobi. Woah! Shola Ameobi. Knees bend, arms stretched. Ra! Ra! Ra!"

The Geordie striker gets the 'Hokey Cokey' treatment

"I'm dreaming of a white Christmas. Just like the ones I used to know. Where the three points glisten. Their strikers are missing. And we see Habib score a goal."

Fans hail Habib Beye to the tune of 'White Christmas'

THE FUNNIEST FOOTBALL CHANTS... EVER!

"There's only one Faustino Asprilla. When he does a cartwheel, you know he's scored a thriller. He'll sh*t on United, the 'Pool and the Villa. Tino Asprilla!"

To the tune of 'Macarena'

"He's fat, he's round. He swears like Chubby Brown. Joe Kinnear, Joe Kinnear!"

After his foul-mouthed tirade at a journalist

"Sunday, Monday, Habib Beye. Tuesday, Wednesday, Habib Beye. Thursday, Friday, Habib Beye. Saturday, Habib Beye, rockin' all week with you!"

To the tune of 'Happy Days'

THE FUNNIEST FOOTBALL CHANTS... EVER!

"In the land, where I was born. Lives a man with a monkey's head. And he went to Sunderland. And his name is Peter Reid. Peter Reid's got a f*cking monkey's head. A f*cking monkey's head. A f*cking monkey's head."

The manager gets a chant to the tune of 'Yellow Submarine'

"He makes us sing and he makes us dance. He's our superstar, who comes from France. It's Ginola – la la la Ginola. They say we've got the most fanatical fans. And we've also got Les Ferdinand. And Ginola – la la la Ginola."

David Ginola gets a version of 'Lola' by the Kinks

THE FUNNIEST FOOTBALL CHANTS... EVER!

NOTTINGHAM FOREST

"Darren, call your dad. Darren, Darren, call your dad!"

Directed at Peterborough manager Darren Ferguson

"Andy Impey's got no neck, got no neck, got no neck. Andy Impey's got no neck. Poor old Andy."

A ditty for the midfielder

"He's big, he's fast. His first name should come last. Stern John, Stern John."

A witty Forest chant

"What's that coming over the hill, is it Assombalonga?"

Forest fans on Britt Assombalonga

"Cheer up Andy Reid. Oh, what can it mean. To be better than Giggsie, in a great football team."

A 'Daydream Believer' remix for the winger

"My garden shed, my garden shed. Is bigger than this, is bigger than this. It's got a door and a window. My garden shed is bigger than this."

The Forest faithful away at Rotherham

"A shot, he's missed, he must be rather drunk…"

The fans adapt their chant after Brian Clough asked them not to swear

"You must have come on a skateboard."

Forest fans to Yeading's support of 60 in the FA Cup

SOUTHAMPTON

"He went for a sh*t, he went for a sh**t. Jason Puncheon, he went for a sh*t."

After Jason Puncheon re-emerged from the dressing room after a quick visit

THE FUNNIEST FOOTBALL CHANTS... EVER!

"You're just a theme park in Preston."

Saints fans to their Blackpool counterparts

"He's got a pineapple on his head!"

Laughing at Charlton's Zheng Zhi

"Have you got another kit?"

Sung to Man United a year after Alex Ferguson blamed their grey strip for losing

Chelsea fans: "Champions League, you'll never win that."

Southampton fans: "Johnstone's Paint Trophy, you'll never win that!"

THE FUNNIEST FOOTBALL CHANTS... EVER!

"Posh Spice is a slapper, her knickers smell of cod. And when she's sh*gging Beckham, she thinks of Ormerod!"

Saints fans get fishy

"We're all standing on a future block of flats."

Southampton fans at Fratton Park

"Knowing me, knowing you, Pa-hars!"

The Saints laud Marians Pahars

"Your bird's too fit for you."

For Stoke's Peter Crouch, who is married to model Abbey Clancy

THE FUNNIEST FOOTBALL CHANTS... EVER!

"What time's your minibus?"

To the handful of Hartlepool supporters

TOTTENHAM

"P*ss in a bottle. You couldn't p*ss in a bottle."

After Rio Ferdinand missed a drugs test

"Why's the mascot on the pitch?"

A chant at a diminutive Wigan substitute

"Hey, hey, Scousers, ooh, ah! I wanna know. Where my car has gone..."

Tottenham fans at Anfield

THE FUNNIEST FOOTBALL CHANTS... EVER!

"Your suit's from Matalan. Your suit's from Matalan. Your suit's from Matalan. Your suit's from Matalan..."

In response to the Chelsea chant, 'Jose Mourinho, Jose Mourinho'

"Super Luka, nuts are we – we're all Luka loopy!"

Saluting Luka Modric, to the tune of Chas & Dave's 'Snooker Loopy'

"You're dead, and you know you are. You're dead, and you know you are..."

Sung to Leicester striker Elvis Hammond

THE FUNNIEST FOOTBALL CHANTS... EVER!

"Sit down Pinocchio. Sit down Pinocchio..."
Directed at manager Gareth Southgate

"Sing when you're farming. You only sing when you're farming..."
The Tottenham faithful at Norwich

"Oh Ledley Ledley. He's only got one knee. He's better than John Terry. Oooh Ledley Ledley..."
Ode to Ledley King

"You're just a sh*t Chas & Dave."
Spurs fans to Liam and Noel Gallagher

THE FUNNIEST FOOTBALL CHANTS... EVER!

WEST HAM

"He's coming for you, he's coming for you. Harry Potter, he's coming for you."
To the bald midfielder Jonjo Shelvey who resembles Lord Voldemort

"He's got a bird's nest on his head."
Sung to Everton's Marouane Fellaini

"Who's the midget in the suit?"
Vertically-challenged Bolton manager Sammy Lee gets a chant from the fans

THE FUNNIEST FOOTBALL CHANTS... EVER!

"Does your butler know you're here?"

West Ham supporters to the 'posh' Fulham ones at Craven Cottage

"If you made a lot of money selling biscuits, buy our club."

Singing to the tune of the Club biscuit commercial in tribute to biscuit baron Eggert Magnusson

"When you're sat in row Z, and the ball hits your head, that's Zamora!"

Fans taunt striker Bobby Zamora

THE FUNNIEST FOOTBALL CHANTS... EVER!

"His name is Rio and he watches from the stand."

On defender Rio Ferdinand, to the tune of Duran Duran's 'Rio', after he was banned for missing a drugs test

"We can see you. We can see you. We can see you holding hands!"

At Brighton, referring to the town's standing as the gay capital of England

"We've got Di Canio, you've got our stereos."

Hammers supporters away at Liverpool

THE FUNNIEST FOOTBALL CHANTS... EVER!

WOLVES

"One Rodney Trotter. There's only one Rodney Trotter."

A chant for Peter Crouch

"Oh Joao Moutinho. He loves a vino. He came from Monaco, to Wanderers. He's five foot seven. He's football heaven. So please don't take Moutinho away..."

Paying tribute to the Portuguese midfielder

"There's only one Jimmy Krankie!"

Directed at Leeds boss Dennis Wise

THE FUNNIEST FOOTBALL CHANTS... EVER!

"He's Korean. He's only on loan for a season. We all think that he's brilliant. He's Hwang Hee-chan."

The striker's chant to the tune of 'She's Electric' by Oasis

"Patrick Cutrone, Patrick Cutrone. He loves the pizza, he loves the pasta. The lad's f*cking magic."

The Italian later said: "It was a nice chant, but I never told them I don't like pizza."

"Jeff Shi, went to Spain. In a Lamborghini. He brought us back a manager. Julen Lopetegui..."

A ditty for the Wolves chairman

THE FUNNIEST FOOTBALL CHANTS... EVER!

"All you do is. All you do is. All you do is wash your hair!"

A chant for striker Andy Keogh

"You can stick your f*cking tower up your a*se."

Sung away at Blackpool

"Tina, Tina, give us a wave!"

Directed David James' 'Tina Turner' afro at Portsmouth

CELTIC

"If you cannae beat the Ajax, beat your wife."

Taunting Rangers supporters

"In your Monaco slums. You look through the dustbins for something to eat. You find a dead lobster and think it's a treat. In your Monaco slums."

An away day at the wealthy Monaco

"Let's all go to Tesco. Where Rangers buy their best clothes. Na na na na."

Taunting the arch rivals

"He is D, he's delightful. He is I, he's incredible. He is C, he's for Celtic. He is A, he's amazing. He is N, he's a natural. He is I, he's Italian. He is O, O, O! D I Canio! D I Canio!"

The fans' version of Ottawan's 'D.I.S.C.O.'

THE FUNNIEST FOOTBALL CHANTS... EVER!

"There's only one Nakamura. There's only one Nakamura. He eats chow mein. He votes Sinn Fein. Walking in a Naka wonderland!"

The Japanese star gets a unique chant

"He's tall, he's skinny, he's going to Barlinnie."

When ex-Rangers' star Duncan Ferguson was sent to jail

"Charlie Adam's sister's pants are the best. You can smell them from the east to the west. They are better when soiled and damp. Charlie Adam's sister's pants!"

Chant for the Rangers player, to the tune of 'Stars and Stripes Forever'

THE FUNNIEST FOOTBALL CHANTS... EVER!

"Last Christmas I gave you my heart, but the very next day, you gave it away. This year, to save me from tears, I'll give it to Postecoglou."

Paying tribute to the manager with the theme of Wham's 'Last Christmas'

RANGERS

"He saves on the left, he saves on the right. Allan McGregor, sh*gs 10 birds a night."

Saluting the goalkeeper

"Georgios Samaras. You're just a woman with a beard!"

Mocking the Celtic forward

THE FUNNIEST FOOTBALL CHANTS... EVER!

"Two Andy Gorams. There's only two Andy Gorams."

Hailing their keeper who was suffering with mild schizophrenia

"They tried to make me sign for Celtic, but I said no, no, no!"

A chant about Steven Naismith to the tune 'Rehab' by Amy Winehouse

"Nakamura ate my dog, ate my dog. Nakamura ate my dog, ate my dog. He sliced him and he diced him. He fried him in a wok. Nakamura ate my dog."

To Celtic's Shunsuke Nakamura

"There's only one Jorge Cadete. He's got hair like spaghetti. He's Portuguese. He's one of these [rude hand gesture]. Walking in a Laudrup wonderland."
Mocking Celtic's Portuguese striker

"Deep-fry your vodka. We're gonna deep-fry your vodka. Deep-fry your vodka!"
To Zenit St Petersburg fans

"Tsamina mina, eh eh. Fashion Jnr, eh eh. Tsamina mina zangalewa. He comes from Zambia!"
Fashion Sakala's song to the tune of Shakira's 'Waka Waka'

THE FUNNIEST FOOTBALL CHANTS... EVER!

BIRMINGHAM

"Fahey's a jolly good fellow. Fahey's a jolly good fellow. Fahey's a jolly good fellow. And so say all of us!"

Keith Fahey's witty chant

BLACKBURN

"It's just like watching The Bill!"

Sang to the lines of police at Ewood Park

BOLTON

"You're just a fat Spanish waiter."

To Liverpool manager Rafa Benitez

BURY

"His name's a department store. You know he's gonna score."

Praising striker Lenny John-Lewis

CHARLTON

"We all agree, Asda is better than Harrods."

Chant at Mohamed Al Fayed-owned Fulham

COLCHESTER

"We can't see you sneaking out!"

Chanting to Southampton fans whose side were 2-0 down as freezing fog descended over the stadium

THE FUNNIEST FOOTBALL CHANTS... EVER!

DUNDEE

"You are a weegie. A smelly weegie. You're only happy on giro day. Your mum's out stealing. Your dad's out dealing. Please don't take my hubcaps away!"
Dundee fans to their United counterparts

FALKIRK

"Cedric, Cedric, show us Uras."
To French defender Cedric Uras

GRIMSBY

"P*ss on your fish. Yes we do, yes we do!"
Retort to: "You only sing when you're fishing."

THE FUNNIEST FOOTBALL CHANTS... EVER!

HIBERNIAN

"When the Hibs go up, to lift the Scottish Cup, we'll be dead. We'll be dead."
After losing in the Scottish Cup Final

HUDDERSFIELD

"We've got Novak. We've got Novak. Our carpets are filthy. We've got Novak!"
Lee Novak gets a clever chant

IPSWICH

"You're Camp and you know you are."
To QPR keeper Lee Camp

MIDDLESBROUGH

"One Job on Teeside. There's only one Job on Teeside!"
Hailing Joseph-Desire Job

MILLWALL

"What's it like to stink of fish?"
Lions fans away at Grimsby

MK DONS

"We all agree, Easter is better than Christmas."
After Jermaine Easter netted against Stockport on Boxing Day

THE FUNNIEST FOOTBALL CHANTS... EVER!

NORWICH

"Yousef's here and Yousef's there, here we go, Moroccan all over the world."

Yousef Safri is 'Rockin' All Over the World'

OLDHAM

"Give us a T (T). Give is an I (I). Give us a T (T). Give us an S (S). What do you do with 'em? Old-em!"

A clever chest chant

PORTSMOUTH

"He comes from Zimbabwe, he'll score eventually!"

A chant for striker Benjani

PORT VALE

"You're supposed to be a gnome!"

Aimed at a particularly short referee

QPR

"Strawberry blond, you're having a laugh."

To Palace's red-haired midfielder Ben Watson

READING

"You should have gone Christmas shopping."

Sang with the Royals 4-0 up against Bristol City

SCUNTHORPE

"Who needs Mourinho? We've got our physio."
When club physio Nigel Adkins was appointed caretaker manager

SHEFF WEDS

"He's big, he's Scouse, he looks like Mickey Mouse – it's Franny Jeffers, Franny Jeffers!"
Serenading their forward

STEVENAGE

"You're going home in a combine harvester."
Having a laugh at the Exeter fans

STOKE

"You're just a fat Maradona."
Taunting Carlos Tevez

STOCKPORT

"There's only on Carlton Palmer. And he smokes marijuana. He's six foot tall. His head's too small. Living in a Palmer wonderland."
A ditty for the manager

SUNDERLAND

"He's big, he's thick, he's got a ginger d*ck. Paul McShane, Paul McShane."
A unique chant for the Irishman

WATFORD

"We should have stayed at the fun fair."

After going 2-0 down at Southend

WIGAN

"We won it two times. We won it two times. Auto Windscreens, we've won it two times."

Responding to Liverpool's "We won it three times" chant

WREXHAM

"Oh fluffy sheep, are wonderful. Oh fluffy sheep, are wonderful. Because they're white and they're Welsh. Oh fluffy sheep, are wonderful."

The fans own the Welsh stereotype

THE FUNNIEST FOOTBALL CHANTS... EVER!

ENGLAND

"Just one Capello, give him to me. Delicious manager, from Italy!"
England fans welcome the new manager at Wembley

"Oh I'd rather be a turnip than a Swede. Oh I'd rather be a turnip. Rather be a turnip. Rather be a turnip than a Swede."
Taunting the Swedish fans

"5-1, even Heskey scored."
Celebrating the famous win over Germany

THE FUNNIEST FOOTBALL CHANTS... EVER!

"Oh, Harry Maguire's magic. He wears a magic hat. And if you throw a brick at him. He'll head the f*cker back. He heads it to the left. He heads it to the right. And when we win the Euros, we'll sing this song all night!"

A tribute to the centre half

"He's big, he's bad, he dances like my dad. Peter Crouch! Peter Crouch!"

Saluting the forward

"His name is Rio, and he should be in the stands!"

After Rio Ferdinand made an error in Ukraine

THE FUNNIEST FOOTBALL CHANTS... EVER!

"You're just a sh*t Andy Carroll."

Directed at Sweden's Zlatan Ibrahimovic

"Does your mummy know you're here?"

To Egypt fans at Wembley

"Oh they should have built a wall, not a bridge. They should have built a road and not a bridge."

The Three Lions fans in Wales

"You're sh*t, but your birds are fit. You're sh*t, but your birds are fit."

Sung to Ukraine in Dnipro

THE FUNNIEST FOOTBALL CHANTS... EVER!

NORTHERN IRELAND

"We love our itsy bitsy, teeny weeny. Baldy headed, Warren Feeney. Plays in Dundee and he can't score a goal!"

Sang to the tune of 'Yellow Polka Dot Bikini' in Slovenia

"Away in a manger. No room for a bed. The little Lord Jesus lay down his sweet head. The stars in the bright sky looked down where... Healy! Healy! Healy!"

The well-known Christmas carol, David Healy style

THE FUNNIEST FOOTBALL CHANTS... EVER!

"Will Griggs on fire, your defence is terrified. Will Griggs on fire. Na, na, na, na…"

The unofficial anthem of Euro 2016 to the tune of 'Freed From Desire'

"He's tall, he's thin, he looks like Jimmy Quinn. He's Jimmy Quinn."

The new Quinn is actually the old one

"Artur Boruc, Ulster's number one!"

Mocking the Celtic keeper after a howler at Windsor Park

THE FUNNIEST FOOTBALL CHANTS... EVER!

"You are my Davis. My Steven Davis. You make me happy, when skies are grey. So f*ck your Lampard and Steven Gerrard. But please don't take my Davis away."

A ditty for the midfielder

"We're not Brazil, we're Northern Ireland and it's all the same to me."

The popular self-deprecating song

"You can stick your flat-pack wardrobes up your a*se."

At at away fixture in Sweden

THE FUNNIEST FOOTBALL CHANTS... EVER!

REPUBLIC OF IRELAND

"Alive, alive-o-oh. Alive, alive-o-oh. Stephen Ireland's two grannies. Alive, alive-oh!"

A song for the midfielder after he pretended one granny, then the other was dead to excuse himself from playing

"All you need is Duff, da da da da da. All you need is Duff, da da da da da. All you need is Duff, Duff. Duff is all you need."

Damien Duff gets a catchy song to the tune of The Beatles classic 'All You Need is Love'

"He's sh*gging your wife. He's sh*gging your wife. Jan Vertonghen, he's shagging your wife!"
Ireland fans taunt Christian Eriksen during their match against Denmark

"We've got Wesley, Wesley Hoolahan, I just don't think you understand. The super Irish man, he's better than Zidane, we've got Wesley Hoolahan."
Irish fans' tribute to the midfielder

"Go home to your sexy wives, go home to your sexy wives!"
Banter with the Swedish at Euro 2016, to the tune of 'Go West' by the Pet Shop Boys

THE FUNNIEST FOOTBALL CHANTS... EVER!

"Don't blame it on Staunton, don't blame it on Givens, don't blame it on Keano, blame it on Delaney."

Chanted at FAI chief executive John Delaney, to the tune of 'Blame it on the Boogie'

"We've got Glenn Whelan, and tonight's gonna be a good night!"

Whelan gets his own song, to the tune of 'I've Got A Feeling' by The Black Eyed Peas

"He wears a tea cosy on his head, he's got a big tea cosy on his head."

The Boys in Green salute Stephen Hunt in Prague against the Czechs

SCOTLAND

"One team in Tallinn, there's only one team in Tallinn."

Sang when Estonia failed to show up for the international

"Deep-fry yer pizzas, we're gonna deep-fry yer pizzas."

Scotland supporters in Italy

"Deep-fry yer long boats, we're gonna deep-fry yer long boats."

The Tartan Army in Norway

THE FUNNIEST FOOTBALL CHANTS... EVER!

"He's fat, he's round, ideologically unsound. Kim Jong II, Kim Jong II..."

Supporters against Korea in the Kirin Cup

"We hate Coca-Cola, we hate Fanta too, because we're the Tartan Army and we love Irn Bru!"

The fans can't get enough of the orange fizzy stuff

"He's short, he's fat, he's gonna get the sack, Advocaat!"

Taunting the Holland manager after a 1-0 triumph

THE FUNNIEST FOOTBALL CHANTS... EVER!

"You're only half as good as last time!"

Scotland fans to Holland after conceding a third goal, having lost 6-0 previously

"Big f*cking pylon, it's just a big f*cking pylon!"

Mocking the Eiffel Tower in France

"You only sing karaoke!"

To Japan supporters in Yokohama

"Sing when you're whaling, you only sing when you're whaling!"

Scotland fans at the game with Iceland

THE FUNNIEST FOOTBALL CHANTS... EVER!

WALES

"Oh I'd rather sh*g a sheep than wear a rose. Oh I'd rather sh*g a sheep than wear a rose, rather sh*g a sheep, rather sh*g a sheep than wear a rose."

Mocking England to the tune of 'She'll Be Coming Round the Mountain'

"Don't take me home. Please don't take me home. I just don't wanna go to work. I wanna stay here. And drink all your beer. Please don't, please don't take me home."

The popular anthem of Euro 2016 to the tune of 'Achy Breaky Heart'

THE FUNNIEST FOOTBALL CHANTS... EVER!

"You can stick your chariot up your a*se!"

Welsh fans to their English counterparts

"We hate England, we hate England. We hate England more than you!"

When playing Scotland or Ireland

"Chris Coleman had a dream. To build the national team. We had no strikers so we played with five at the back (five at the back). With Bale in attack (with Bale in attack). Watch out Europe, we're on our way back!"

To the tune of 'Sloop John B' by The Beach Boys

THE FUNNIEST FOOTBALL CHANTS... EVER!

"Ain't nobody like Joe Ledley. Makes me happy, makes me feel this way."

To the theme of 'Ain't Nobody' by Chaka Khan

"Voulez Vous, Conor Roberts on the right. And he plays in red and white, and he's f*cking dynamite."

Sang to the tune of Abba's 'Voulez Vous'

"He's fast, he's quick. His name's a narcotic. Gary Speed, Gary Speed."

A catchy number for the midfielder

Also available

www.ingramcontent.com/pod-product-compliance
Lightning Source LLC
Chambersburg PA
CBHW050304120526
44590CB00016B/2489